Jumbly
Collection of
Wordy Things

Jumbly

Copyright © (Sarah Johnson 2024)
All Rights Reserved

No part of this book may be reproduced in any form by photocopying or any electronic or mechanical means including information storage or retrieval systems, without permission in writing from both the copyright owner and publisher of the book.

ISBN: 9781836022121
Perfect Bound

First published in 2024 by bookvault Publishing, Peterborough, United Kingdom

An Environmentally friendly book printed and bound in England by bookvault, powered by printondemand-worldwide

For Violet

Table of contents

Introduction

Book 1: Grass Stained Book

    Poems

    Songs

    Excerpts

Book 2: The Trick of Limerence

    Part 1: Not Healthy

    Part...then: Still not healthy

    Part Never

    Part - Rock Bottom

    Part Healing

    Part Begi-nding

Book 3: Hope and Grace

Pages waiting for your wordy things

Jumbly once was the name of a cat. Did you know that? Only in the mind of a madman but that madman may have saved the world, as they are occasionally wont to do. Contradiction? Why, yes! And that is only the beginning. Join me for a little while in a strange and tumbly mindscape. It be rumbly tumbly jumbly in here.

Far too unhinged, I cannot lash my cart to only poetry. Herein you will find songs and excerpts from unpublished works, mind ramblings and, yes, quite a few poems that only occasionally care to rhyme. (Any rhyming is almost entirely by accident, I assure you.)

To accompany this publication I have created a reading, with optional commentary, that can be found at https://essee1.bandcamp.com/.

Drink up, my darlings. This cerebral beverage should take you on a ride, if you have the mind.

Book 1:
Grass Stained Book
Lovey-dovey word slinging

Poems

That's it
That's the one
I woke to your silly face
and I was done
All was right
in a the midst of wrong
and I'd never be free
of your sweet song

Dessert First

Frantically
There commenced a scramble
Feet and hands flailing
Toes and fingers gripping for purchase
From prone to running
In a whirl of delighted frenzy
Tackle
Laugh
Then only breathing
Strange sounds
giggled sighs
Then
Only then
catching up

Syntax

The way to her heart was silence.

Music is beautiful and alluring and words are somehow both concrete and fundamentally inadequate.

Moans and purring, while blissful, come attached to fleeting pleasures. Breathing, even, would stop eventually and the heart with its imperfect but implacable rhythm.

No, it was the silent knowing that she craved.
The absence of predictable behavior coupled seamlessly with the inevitability of intention.
He would always choose her.

Her deeply flawed efforts to fulfill iridescent desires. Her absolute need to be better today than yesterday. Her self doubt and paradoxical conceit.

She never knew how or even when but with no sound or preamble he would show her that he wanted it all. All of her into all of him.

The truth of it rang in the impulse. With this gesture or that look. With the lifting of a burden, here, or a letting her carry it on her own so she knew she could, there.

Offering his wound for her, to heal, eyes sparkling at her satisfaction with his relief.

It was never I love you she wanted. It was only love. For the true sound of love is heard in time and choices, never voices.

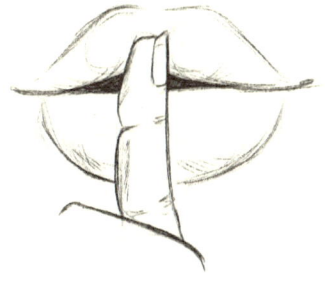

The floor is

Upside down on the couch
like I am four again.

I won't tell you
I can see up your nose
if you promise not to mention
London or France.

Make me laugh 'til I tumble
then come join me
in the lava.

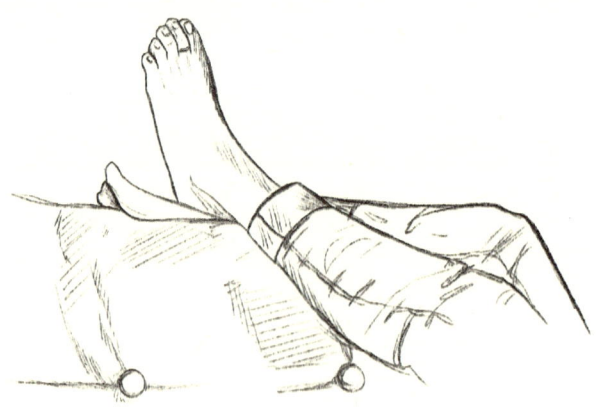

Pulse

I have a pulse that's not my heartbeat
It's the rhythm of your hands
Grasping at my gasping
Rummaging through my senses
Gently teasing twitches
From deep within
Leftovers languishing
While glowing after

I have a pulse that's not my heartbeat
Rising and falling with your breaths
Slipping between your arms
Humming in the wake
Of your release

I have a pulse that's not my heartbeat
Luscious silky sliding
In time with muscles straining
Gripping and pressing and pulling
Quickening then slowing

Finding losing laughing weeping
Timed to a metronome
Passed back and forth
Back and forth
Back and forth

I know nothing but the pulse that's not my heartbeat

Wet

Sitting at coffee with you
When I plumb your depths
If my line runs out
So does my dry spell

No name

My love is a treetop in the wind
Sway and bow and sometimes
Break
But ever growing
Toward the light

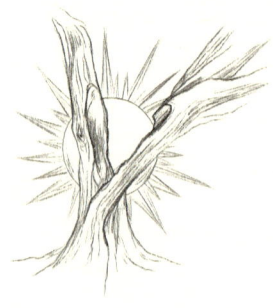

Cloak

Tickling trickling spine dripping
Draws forth seething
Pulsing pressure spewing
Breath halting between moments
Floating somewhere without

Connected tranquil lounging
Beneath oceans of stars
Lapping contented at liquid muscles

Turning over to kiss your mouth
Like I could breathe and drink and eat and taste you
From lifetimes away

This avalanche of moonlight
Cloaking me from God's own sight

Fight

Hands that cover more of me
Than seems possible just resting there
Fingers finding sounds in me
Bringing me to life
Dragging me out of my mind
And into the moment

Teasing stroking
Stoking smoldering Fires within
Steaming thru to the finish
or just riding an endless wave

Silly trickster will love for me
But not fight for me
I'd fight you for you. Why won't you fight me for me?

Heaven's Gate

Bloody memories trickling in
Wandering rivulets in the folds of my brain
Flavor of iron like I'd bit my cheek
But then that thick earthy tang
As though it pulled pleasure from you instead
Salty savor on your nape
Tasting your tongue in a meta awakening
My own saliva
Harolding thirst in me
As yours drips down in between
Tastes change in a mouth suddenly dry
From gasping again and again
Riding your insistence
On thrusting me thru heaven's gate

Short but sweet

I want our story to be a grass stained book
Earthy, dingy pages with doodles on every one
Dog eared corners of our favorite bits
To finger to now and again
Cracked to the smell of you
Because it lay open on your chest a while
As we kissed

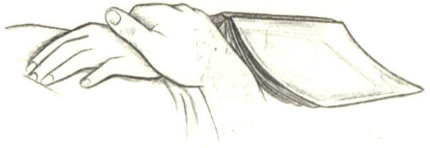

Draw

Draw me in
       Crooked finger and daring eyes
Draw me close
       Chin clamped on shoulder
Draw me out
       Spine traced to beckon shivers
Draw me further
       Stepping from this flesh to greet you
Draw my shadow
       Around you and give me what you desire

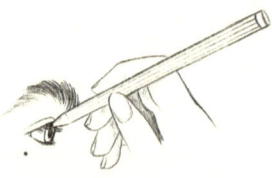

Songs

Asking

Bring it in
Shape it up
Pull the cord
Take it rough

Would it be too much to ask

Light me up
Feel the force
Push and pull
Let it take us

Should it be too much to ask

If I want
Would you let me
If I ask
Would you take me

Well, this is me just basking
This is me…

Li'l Lust Song

I
I wanna kiss your face
I wanna see you smile
When I touch your toes
With my toes
I wanna lift your heart
Into the clouds
And watch it soar
On pleasures wings
I
I wanna touch you
I wanna feel you
I wanna kiss your face

Holiday Song

People are laughing
While frost is creeping
And bakers are
Crafting delights

Spruce and pine wafting
Snowflakes are dancing
Landing so
Softly outside

Voices ringing
Feet prancing
Noses redning
Fingers wiggling in gloves
As breath clouds mingle
While sleigh bells jingle
A tune helping you feel the love

Paper is crinkling
As wreaths are swaying
And candles are
Winking their spark

Tho couples are kissing
The lights they are twinkling
And no one is
Missing the dark.

Let's fill the season
With people and parties
Share it with everyone

But after gifts are opened
Carols are echoed
And feasts are all done

Let's have a cozy, slow,
Quiet evening
Catching up
like we always do

It's been way too long again
I just want to
See you for real
Old friend true

Love Answers

Simple feeling
Rushing in
Complications
Sidling up
To shut it down

But

(Chorus)
Hope calls
And love answers
Grace falls
And finds forever
To see you smile
I'd light a fire
'Til the tips of my fingers remember

Sit here with me
Feel the pull
Giving up love
Is hard enough
Find what's in you

So

Chorus

I know what I feel
Tho there's so many reasons
Can't
Shouldn't
Won't work
Couldn't
But too bad
It's too clear
Take my hand
Embrace fear

Cus

Chorus

One of these days

Just sitting on my heels
Ready to leap
Don't wanna miss it
So I Just don't sleep

(Chorus)
One of these days
I'll know where you've been and
One of these days
I'll know where you wanna go
One of these days
I'll see you there
And you know we'll take it slow-oh

I see you wanna see
I know you wanna know
But I'll be damned
If I trade me for you

So I
Listen for the gun
I'm off like a shot
I'm on my way
Ready or not

Chorus

Excerpts

Excerpt one:

Garret pulled away enough to look at Jenny's face. Her persistent blush of embarrassment had transformed into a glowing flush of arousal. She kept her eyes closed and he saw her lip tremble.

"Oh." was the only sound to escape her.

No one had kissed him like that before. She barely moved her mouth at all, but hadn't needed to. He could feel her anticipation and was sure she would have tried to take it further. She didn't. Instead, she savored what he offered.

Garret exhaled with a soft, low sound from deep in his throat. This was going to be better than he hoped. He draped her arms over his shoulders and put one hand in her hair, the other on her waist. She wrapped her arms around his neck and found his lips again.

They stood there for much longer than he'd originally planned. She had a way of coaxing very subtle movements from him that he found intoxicating. Hands and lips explored tenderly but in ways that avoided the next level. Until he opened his mouth on her neck, below her jaw, just wide enough for his tongue to press hot and wet to her skin.

Her hands, which had been moving up his back, grabbed his shirt as she inhaled sharply in response. Her head relaxed back into the door and she moaned softly. Garret kept his tongue in that spot and sucked ever so slightly. She gripped him harder and he allowed his tongue to undulate subtly. Though his movements were almost imperceptible, she nevertheless responded to each with a slight movement of her body.

Garret found the pace and consistency of her responsiveness entranced him in a way he wanted to last forever. It was going to be a very long night.

Excerpt two:

"I think sometimes," she began in a low voice. "I'm so lucky." He looked up at the ceiling.

"Oh?" He invited her to continue.

"I sometimes feel like...like I am the only one in this world who can talk to who I want. Can touch who I want."

He glanced down and realized her hand was resting next to his cup on the table.

"It has nothing to do with luck." Still resting it on the wall, he turned his head to look at her.

She mirrored his movement to meet his gaze.

"Oh?" She invited him to continue.

"You're ridiculously good at your job." he stated flatly

He almost expected her to be offended or saddened by his remark.

Instead she licked her lips and bit the lower one while holding back a smile.

Her eyes sparkled in the lantern light.

"I know." She looked up at the ceiling and he saw her nostrils flare as she held back a silent giggle.

He let his hand slip from the rim of his cup onto hers.

She closed her eyes and turned her hand over so she could run fingers along his palm and wrist from underneath.

He sighed and closed his eyes as well.

Book 2:
The Trick of Limerence

A memoir. Maybe a warning.

Part 1: Not Healthy

Excerpt one:

The heat of so many bodies was stifling and electrifying at once. Each dancing their own way spun chaos through the crowd. Yet, as they all moved to the same beat, ripples of synchronicity formed here and there. Ophelia reveled in feeling the pulse and play, rhythm and jostle. The music always captured her but being immersed in a sea of others, so caught up in the same joy, amplified its power many times.

Growth from Wishes

Simple is desire
Complex is reward
Steeped in mixed up mire
What you see in dreams
Is never what you're moving toward

If your wish and another's
should coincide
It needs some other barrier
To push against
To reach it
Other than each other

Either within or without
Because stagnation is death
We can compel ourselves
But nature decrees
Growth requires resistance

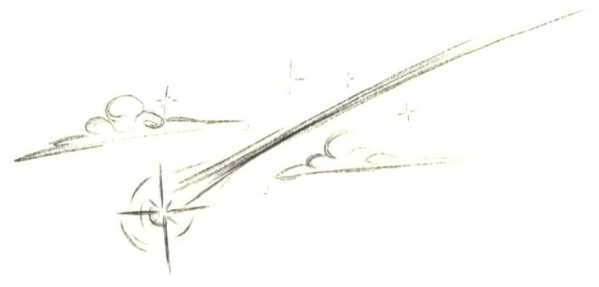

Peek

Surreptitiously I peek
   See
      Smirk in the glint
        Of sea glass eyes
Witness
   Twisting and
      Untwisting
      Helix burning in the dark
Forget
   Light my taper
   And turn to walk away
Think
   'dear God, the price'

Brain Ramblings:

Well shit

This is a very bad time to be dealing with this

I'm not dealing with this.

I can give up the limerence. . . no really

Like I could give up a heroin addiction just cause I decided to…

The hit is too sweet

Like a weird ass mind autoeroticism

So I need to accept my most embarrassing ridiculous parts

Yeah i don't have the tools for that

What do you do when you need help and don't have any or won't accept any cause it's too damned embarrassing

And people would say don't be embarrassed which is stupid cause I am and saying don't when I already do is just more embarrassing so that's not exactly a route out of the hole is it?

Nope just stuck in the shit
Like always

Complaining about petty problems when other people have is so much worse than me

I think I'm depressed

I think life gives you the very best and the very worst at the same time so you have the entire range of options to choose from

I'm overwhelmed and I will probably pick my way through it all, like a slog through the bog

But to what end? To make me stronger? Sure but stronger for what?

I decide what matters, I decide where on the spectrum from horrible to great things about life I land.

Who even is this girl?

If I were really just lost in this fantasy why would I ever feel the urge to reach out at all? I mean the fantasy is the rush right so why ruin by trying to bring any of it into reality?

What in the holy {censored} is wrong with me?

Is it actually just a high I feel when I think I feel or am I actually feeling something and that has to be the most messed up thing I've ever thought

Someone please explain to me why I am wasting so much time attention energy on this? It's just self sabotage right? 'ts gotta be.

Gotta be. I look more and more like an old lady every day in the mirror I am sagging and melting maybe I'm trying to fight that. Feel young feel new feel excited

I can find no metric by which I can calculate to anything but pathetic failure. I know that is super depressing and unattractive and something people avoid at all costs but it's true. I just barely get by, doubt myself constantly and haven't contributed anything to the world or the human race of any mention.

I care way way way way too much. And it literally gets me nothing. I've never made any difference that mattered to anything I care about. I've only ever survived. I've never thrived. I've tried, I've tried to look at life that way and feel like I am free and do things that would be considered thriving. I do somethings and i can be kinda thoughtful and intentional about them for a while and it looks like I might be able to get better at it but I can't seem to follow through and I don't know if it is because my brain is broken or because something inside me thinks I am not worth succeeding and what...

...The

{cencored}

Do

I do

About

It

Either

Way?!

Sit and write stupid journal entries when I should be doing pretty much anything else

Sure I'm working on myself

But I feel like I am dashing in circles and then sitting down in defeat just to get up and dash in circles again.

Maybe step one is, don't feed the delusion

The delusion felt good, it actually got you what you wanted short term it is distracting you from what you want long term

Disengage.

Can you

JUST...

Part...then: Still Not Healthy

<u>I'ma Risk It</u>

Watchin myself
Toe the cliff edge
Call of the thrill
Drowns out logic

Everything else
Falls to silence
This Heart's desire
Offers providence

I want it
That makes it
Right enough for now
I'ma risk it

Consequences
Are Unseen or
Unrecognized
Wandering out there

This little body
Will never know
Better look out
Look out below

I Can't learn it
If I don't chance it

I want it
That makes it
Right enough for now
I'ma risk it

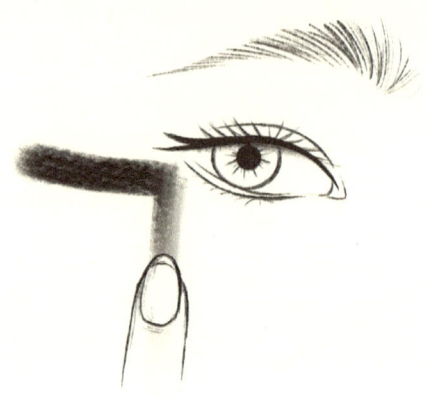

Surrender

Sweet Surrender
Come what may
You are my Rome
It wasn't built in a day
But it will surely burn
Will I fiddle?
Let it light my way?
You can find me, filthy
But content
Playing in the ashes

Vulnerable

I lie supine
Hand on neck
Guarding?
Begging?
I don't know which
Seen too much
Can't go back
Toes grip grass
And pull
And wait
You channel thru a crystal
I thru the earth
Countless life between me
And you
A wave of will
Rides them all
To get to you
To ask you a question
To pull back the curtain

Excerpt two:

Ophelia froze, mid-bite. He gave no sign that he understood how insane his question sounded to her.

Ophelia swallowed, carefully. She set her fork down. Her heart felt a little restricted and sped its pace to compensate. She felt the slight pressure and distant ringing in her ears that told her she was on the verge of a panic attack.

"I, uh…" she began as she rose from the table. "I have to go…my friends…" she sputtered, fumbling for an excuse to leave before the hyperventilation could set in.

"Oh, God, I'm sorry." Greg rose from his seat and came around the table toward her, recognition of her plight clear on his face.

Phee instinctively held out a hand to keep him at arm's length but she lost control of her breathing at that moment and had to grip the back of her chair and the table to keep her balance as she swayed dizzily.

Greg knelt down before her at the distance she'd indicated and looked up into her eyes with a worried expression. He spoke in a low, resonant voice.

"It's alright. I won't touch you. You are safe. Sit down so you don't fall and we'll breathe it out together. Alright?" He gestured for her to sit back in her chair. She did so slowly, sitting sideways on the chair, facing him with her hands still gripping its back and the table.

Phee's body screamed at her to flee, but Greg's voice was level and soothing enough to get through.

He began to mimic her breathing until they were in perfect sync. He then began to alter his own breaths, slowing the timing and steadying the pattern of inhale and exhale. He did this in patient, successive steps, waiting for her to match him at each stage.

Normally, staring into someone's eyes while trying to calm herself would have been wholly counter productive but Greg had clearly done this before. He was obviously doing his own inner mantra to keep very relaxed and level. Phee found he soothed her in a way she'd never experienced before.

It took a few minutes, but Phee was able to get her breathing back under control with his help.

"I put you on the spot. I'm sorry." Greg begged her forgiveness with the most heart-melting half smile and raised eyebrows.

Between feeling so utterly embarrassed and inwardly gushing over his sheer adorableness, Phee felt tears well up behind her eyes. She looked down and let her hair fall over her face, trying to hide them.

Greg leaned in a little.

"You can head to the bathroom if you want to cry in private?" He whispered.

"Or we can hug it out." he added.

Phee let out something between a sob and a laugh. She looked at him, sure he was only joking.

His face was a picture of consolation and he held up arms toward her. He was serious.

Part Never:

Neverland

Cresting with the wave
dissipating and sliding
slipping back into something frothy but cohesive
Rolling again at the call of the moon
toward the sun kissed sand
Reach, reach
grip
slip
pulled back into the depths
Leave me to roll and tumble in and out of the breakers
Bashing and crashing until
Seaglass eyes fix on my mouth
Conch ears hear my reasons
Salty skin blessed with starlight
Feels the tale drip in
Then I'll sink or swim
Sink into you
Or swim to Neverland
Either way I'm free

Cycles

Platitudes and litanies
Chatter and puff
But nothing changes
And everything changes
Cycles seem to wrench me onward
But not exactly forward
The ether spills fun
Sometimes but
I am still here
I am still alone

Excerpt three:

Ophelia had to give it to him. His timing was perfect. They rounded a copse of trees and at the top of the beach near the treeline was a firepit, already lit, and a blanket laid with a picnic.

"I ordered the full-service, deluxe package. They set it up just before we got here." Greg explained.

Phee stopped and put both hands over her mouth.

Greg stood admiring her reaction.

"You bastard." Phee lowered her hands just enough to hiss.

Greg chuckled uneasily.

"This is too much." she went on, "I'm not worth…"

Greg grasped her hand and pulled her into a run toward the blanket.

"Don't do that." he laughed at her while trotting backwards so he could talk to her on the way. "Just come have fun."

When they reached the blanket he grasped her other hand and pulled her down to sit on it.

"No, seriously. I'm just not the kind of person you do this for…" she carried on, wide eyed.

"That's bullshit." Greg was still smiling ear to ear, but his eyes had taken on a steely quality.

His expletive snapped her out of her self deprecating trance and she looked at him.

"You can just enjoy it, Phee." his eyes softened and effortlessly drew her into the moment.

Phee huffed a little breath through her nose and half smiled, sheepish. Then she nodded once.

"You're right. Thanks."

Greg looked satisfied.

"I didn't know what you liked so there's wine and beer in the cooler." he began and started pulling stuff out of the basket between them.

"I don't drink, actually." Phee told him and leaned over the basket to peer inside as well.

"Okay, pretty sure…" he popped the cooler open. "Yep, there's water and…milk in here for some reason."

"Chocolate cake." Phee explained and pulled the cake container out to show him.

"Yeah, I guess that makes sense." he chuckled.

"Um, the barbeque is tonight, right?" Phee eyed all the food he was pulling out.

Greg nodded.

"I got the deluxe package more for the choices than the volume." he explained but looked a little overwhelmed too.

"Heh, maybe I went a l-ee-ttle overboard." he put his finger and thumb close together in front of his face. Phee laughed.

Valentine

I kinda hate Valentine's Day
But it isn't what you think
I'm not lonely
I'm waiting
I'm waiting
I'm waiting
For something
That ain't coming
Kinda hate Valentine's Day
I think I see it
I kinda feel it
I know
I know I'll be okay
But just today
Just today
Will you put me
Put me out of my misery
On this Valentine's Day

Ring me

You ooo ooo ooo
Ring me like a bell
Bring me like a spell
Get me overwhelmed

I aye-yi-aye
Quiver when you look
Shiver on your hook
Lead with my back foot

Bring me in
Lead me on
I'm not strong
You're not wrong

I'll never know where I stand
So I'm sittin' on my hands

Let me in and see
I'm serendipity

Part - rock bottom

Ten things I hate about

I hate
how you distract me and make me feel insane
how the only time you looked in my direction, I felt stupid
how you drew me in with the crowd like a sucking wound
that has yet to heal
that you are always in sight but also out of reach
that I wanted to make beautiful music with you...
like Pepé Le Pew
your wicked smile that melts my flesh to my bones
your voice for no good reason, just because it reminds me
of you
how words come spilling from the ether like you are some
kind of trap door to that place
that I miss you, and that makes less sense than the rest of
it combined

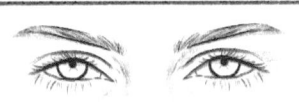

Mind the gap

There's a gap
Between this stalwart heart
On the sturdy platform
And the charging train of runaway desire
There in the void
I could hide where no one would ever suspect
So intent are they on moving from one to the other
    Step right over me
    Where I crouch
    And watch and wait and scowl
    And scootch, reluctantly
    To make room for you

Sometimes

Sometimes I really really want you
And I don't like it
'Cause it makes no sense
But I kinda like it too
'Cause it makes no sense
I love this swirling dance in my head
But I'd rather get off the ride
Then hold you in this limerence
There's no way out
Gotta beat it down
To make it make sense
Love's so stupid
This heart doesn't need a reason
This gut is full of holes
Like the plot of a bad movie
Body want to give
But it's leaving me in the dust

Part: Healing

Soon

Countless Lives
  Stardust dancing upon this sphere
    Weaving in and out
     Coming and going
      I'll see you soon
       She whispered
        As he let go

Bring it

I can be witchy good
I can be bitchy bad
I'll light up goochie goo
I know it makes you mad

Chorus:
Just bring it
Just bring it on
We got this
We got it goin' on

Just bring it
Just bring it up
We'll surface
We'll surf right over this

Just bring it
Bring it to me
We'll swing it
Just wait and see

I see you eyein' me
Why don't you speak your peace
My ladies here for me
So you can let it be

Chorus

We sisters in the dark
We gonna make that mark
Bring it in ma boo
Know I got your back too

Chorus plus

Just bring it
Just bring it on over
We'll holler
Link arms and call RED ROVER

(Refrain shuffled chorus)

Excerpt Four:

"This isn't going to be pretty, no matter what. You don't want to see Greg like that. And besides, there's always the next life...apparently." Phee began to shrug.

"That's bullshit!" Meg's exclamation rang in Phee's ears. She said it exactly the way Greg had, so long before, her eyes steely with absolute certainty.

"But, Meg, if all this is true then—"

"No!" Meg put up a hand to stop Phee from continuing. "I don't care. Even if it is all true. Even if we might have infinite incarnations, don't you dare let that be an excuse to devalue this one."

There was Meg, Phee thought gratefully, bringing sense to the chaos.

"You're right." Phee finally let her tears slip down her cheeks. "I've never been exactly like this before and you'll never be perfect Meg again."

"Well, I don't know about that." Meg's eyes softened as Phee showed she understood. "We're all perfect, really." She smiled a little.

Phee rolled her eyes.

"Perfectly imperfect?" She shook her head slightly. "That never made sense to me."

"It just means," Meg pulled her into another hug. "Perfectly on our way."

Phee hugged her friend back.

"On our way where?" she croaked softly through her tears.

"Wherever we want. That is the point."

Phee nodded into Meg's shoulder, but she wasn't quite sure she really understood. It was just comforting and she trusted the sentiment because it came from Meg.

Part Begi-nding:

Poetic Rambling:

The Sonic Brand

She thought of his face and smiled.

Sometimes she could see it clearly, despite her almost complete aphantasia. If she concentrated, and if the circumstances in her twisted, broken brain were just so, she could conjure it almost clearly. The thought of him in general was enough to set her beaming but she especially liked when she could actually see him there. Smiling wickedly in her mind. She smiled back and wished again that she could do more than just imagine it.

It began innocently enough. She began trying, in her very juvenile and socially awkward way, to interact with others who liked the public work as much as she. That made sense to her. If she could find friends, it would be among others who loved what she loved. That seemed sensible. Of course it was not. There commenced over- sharing and uncomfortable intensity, as aways, until she left in a huff one day (regretting it almost immediately but too embarrassed to return) and that was that.

Except it wasn't, because by then she was already hooked. Even though she didn't have long experience with the rituals or anything, the public forum did something to her. It was a strange mixup of the feelings the public work had stirred in her and the unique experience of the live interaction and the feeling... the feeling.

It was hard to even describe as a feeling. It was more like a frequency. Do you feel a frequency? Hear it beyond hearing? Detect?

In any case, once she'd detected it, something changed inside her. All the feelings she had and bravery she'd dove into in those months before, culminated in a strange awakening at that forum. A definite turning point. And he somehow became the focus.

And through it all, as much as she wanted the frequency to go away, it just wouldn't. It rings in her now, at this moment, and won't let go. She tried focusing on the important things in her life. She tried denying herself any reminders. She tried gently letting herself have glimpses but to approach with a sense of letting go instead of clinging on. Through it all the frequency rang in her still. Just as clear and crisp and undeniable as the day at the forum when it had first been struck.

She is building a new mechanism however, and the hope is that she can use the materials from the old one to make the new. Then, one day, she will look up and the limerence will just be gone. Absorbed into the new, reasonable, functional-outside-someone-else, thing she's built from her own love of self.

She's been on a journey. This poor person, unknowingly, stowed in the little red wagon she is dragging along in her wake.

Still, despite all this, the storm and turmoil and uncertainty and clinging to the certainty that there is nothing there but her crazy -

She thought of his face and smiled.

So young

Every stretch mark
A tally of days
Giving your body to another

Each spot a memory
Of life warmed by the sun

Those crows feet
Etched from countless smiles
That lifted countless souls

Lines on the brow
Deeply worn by worry
Testify of love

Cherish this tome
etched in flesh

When you are ancient as the stars
You will look back
And think

How sweet a story
I wrote with my body
When I was so young.

Purring

Leopurred spots stand out
Against the sky
Under the weight of this sun
I see the mirage
It melts and only I
Am left
Fingers woven
Through fur and snow

Excerpt Five:

"If you let go." She began slowly, to be sure he understood. "We can be together now."

A war of guilt and loss played out on his face.

"Do you love me?" she asked pointedly. Greg nodded with a look that said he was surprised she had to ask.

"Do you love me? Phee? Not the past lives, not the ones to come, me, here, now?" she gripped his face and held his gaze intensely. Greg blinked a couple of times, considering. He nodded, the tears returning.

"Then show me. Show me I am more important to you than the guilt of the past or any promise of a future. Right now, show me that this, right here, is the most important thing to you."

Greg's dawning understanding bloomed on his face like a sunrise.

"Let go." she begged.

Finally:

I will
> Stay curious
> Know my own worth
> And not react like I am going to lose
> any of it Because of what you do
> Be compassionate
> Without shame or making excuses
> That is the very core of me
> And
> I am allowed to show it

Book 3: Hope and Grace
Everything we need is in reach

Pet

    Pet the page to pull the cord
            Curtain swings and lights fade
                    Gratefully catch words that pour into
                          My upturned apron
                          Like a hammock
                                  Toss and settle them gently

    Eyes flick to your face
            Beaming
                Asking
                      If I spill them out before you
                            Will you sift them with me?

    We'll lounge on bellies
            Chins on hands
                Feet dangling upwards
                      Fidgeting in Sheer delight
                          Crafting Jostling Composing through
                          the night

'Til we can't keep our eyes open and laugh ourselves to sleep

Prism blasted sunrise startles away dreaming
Minds at work in moonlight rouse
And offer new paths to explore

Our sustenance, creation
Our pleasure, genesis
All the world seems incidental beyond the ones we birth
Together
In the lava

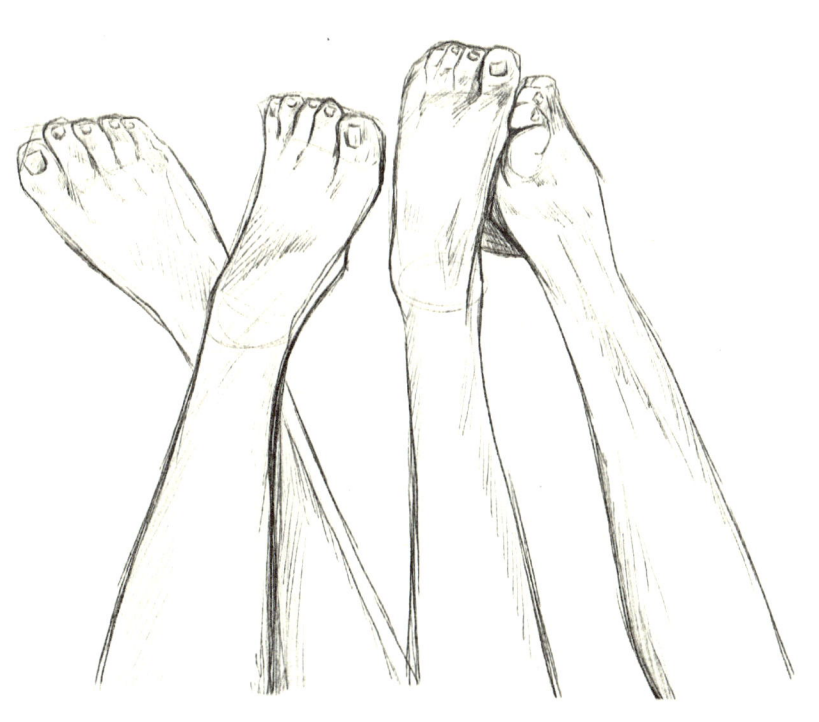

Stained Glass Soul

Eyes flick across skittering flecks of color
Glowing, dancing, bowing over pews
Skewing prayers and bouncing off of
Heads and hands
Shadows blurring colors next to knees
Bent to dust the humble stones
Prismed broken light crosses rainbows
Over lamentations of filtered hues
Stories splashed over supplicant patrons
Propaganda, to bend the unknowable into
Ultimatums for control
But shines far greater light of hope and love
Squinting to escape closed eyelids
Squeezing out between fingers clasped in desperation
May we shatter the windows of broken color
Break down the so called sanctuaries
That are only prisons, citadels
And at last look to the
Wondrous lumination
Of the
Stained Glass Soul

Thank you for your patience

Sitting here just being me
Waiting to coalesce enough to move again
Each step seems to fracture me
So it's easier to do nothing at all
'Til I can stand
To fracture again
Now and then I reach flow
And in those moments
My torn apart state
Becomes harmonious
Glowing helix
A wave in time
Joining dynamically
With all the ripples around me
But mostly i just feel
Like breaks in the smooth surface
A disturbance
To be patiently waited out

Nice things

Sparkly but wasteful
Rare but useless
Sleek but lifeless
Ugly but helpful
Dirty but alive
Common but
Abundant
    Additive
        Uplifting
This is why we can't have nice things

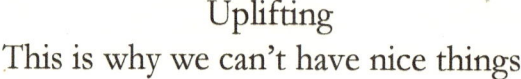

I am

I am air

Best allowed to come and go unbidden

I Allow your fire to burn

But you will Consume me and dance away to light the path of another

having never known I was inside you

I do not give
I surround and fill everything in my path

I cannot hold you up unless you fight me

You will never see me

I am air

Brain ramblings:

You must pass through agony without losing your sense of self.

***

It is because the boundary is not a line. It is a continuum influenced by innumerable factors that must be felt through experience rather than governed by rules.

***

Life has no meaning - until it does.

I came across a reddit thread under r/nostupidquestions that had to do with the purpose of humans in the ecosystem. There weren't that many answers and the reason was clear. They were all wrong but went down a dead end track of thought that would make you think twice about arguing. Not because it can't be argued. It is just one of those thought processes where your reasoning hits a huge, bleak wall and your head hurts for a second from running into it. It makes you want to run away rather than stay and try to get around it.

The answers were like, there is no purpose to anything, including humans and if there is any purpose of all life it is to make more of itself and that is all.

All I could think was, "Jeesh, depressed much?"

You have to chuckle (otherwise you'd weep) for those poor souls, squandering their humanity to oblivion like that. I mean, follow my reasoning here. We have consciousness. Within that consciousness we create meaning and assign purpose. The purpose of humans is to be conscious of purpose.

This is where your brain starts to do mental cartwheels and the meaning of words feels fuzzy. Well, squeeze your eyes and shake your head a bit and come back to reality. I'll try not to do that again but, well, words don't actually work for a lot of things we try to communicate. Let's just accept that and move on.

If life only exists because it can, then it can make us, we can make purpose, therefore life can have purpose. *mic drop*

But seriously, I hope you're starting to understand where I am going with this. For a human to type the words "there is no purpose," it's like a flower telling the bee, "there is no pollen." If the bee shrugs and buzzes off to a more accommodating flower, the first flower doesn't reproduce and hasn't fulfilled its core directive. If all life only responds in ways that make it procreate better, then how is the ability to be conscious of the concept of purpose helping us procreate?

Are we breaking the mold? With greater and greater complexity of biology - by which I am mainly referring to our massive brains - do we deviate from this directive somehow?

Or are we reproductive cells of the superorganism that is Earth? Tipping the balance for a species that can exploit resources on such a grand scale as to be able to leave the planet and seed others.

Neil deGrasse Tyson once talked about intelligence and compared us to our nearest biological relatives. Then he talked about trying to imagine life that was that degree more intelligent than ourselves. I love how everyone always jumps straight to "Ha! Nefarious Aliens" and no one thinks, "Oh good, something to aspire to."

What I am trying to say is, stop negating your own superpowers, people. If you understand the word "purpose", you can find it. You'll never reach any further if you don't reach at all. Go find it.

Excerpt last:

"Why do you fondle that thing?" Jhoppa smirked as Keller dropped the scroll case almost guiltily. Keller grimaced and reached for it again.

"I can't understand how it was crafted. I've never seen anything like it." Forgetting himself Keller again began to run his fingers slowly across its surface, willing himself to feel the seams between wood and metal but, as always, his fingers could not detect where exactly one met the other, only that one was a bit colder in the night air.

Jhoppa sniffed.

"I'd wager a great deal that I could reach from where I sit and find something you've never seen." He jabbed the fire stick he'd been prodding up flames with in Keller's direction. "I'll never understand how one could live their whole life in the shadow of one mountain ... much less generations, one after another." Jhoppa actually shuddered.

Keller rolled his eyes and tried not to think about his home in too much detail for fear of the knot such thoughts always tied in his stomach.

"But this is from the mountain. It's Robinia wood. It's from the Mountain God."

Jhoppa eyed him, half smiling.

"Keller" the tall traveler began slowly. Keller looked up to meet his gaze. "You realize what you just said?

"It's," he indicated the case, "from a God."

Keller frowned a bit. "So?"

Jhoppa barked a laugh. "So, don't you think your God could turn out a work just a bit," he held his fingers close together, "superior to anything a mortal might produce?"

Keller considered the scroll case and Jhoppa's words carefully. It had never occurred to him that Nayron may have actually made it himself. Keller wasn't aware of shaking his own head.

Jhoppa was staring at him, half incredulous, half amused.

"No? I knew Nayron had a different sort of relationship with his worshippers than most but I'd no idea you held him in such low regard—"

Keller was on his feet before he knew what he was doing. "That's not what I meant!"

Jhoppa held up his hands in mock defense, still smiling. "All right. All right." He spread his hands. "Sit down. What did you mean?"

Keller breathed deeply and sat once more letting the object of their discussion rest in his lap as he collected his thoughts.

"I know I'm young," he began in a mutter "but I've never heard of Nayron making anything."

Jhoppa's grin broadened. Keller waved angrily as though trying to ward off his snide remark before he made it.

"Not that he couldn't..." Keller cast about in his mind to bring together the ends of this thoughts. "It's just," he fumbled on, "he doesn't.

"He doesn't just hand us whatever we need. He would show us how to do it ourselves. Even if it took generations to perfect a craft. With those he favored, he would share secrets so they could work as He might."

Keller ventured a look at his traveling companion. To his surprise Jhoppa's eyes seemed to glow a bit more than the fire light reflecting from them. He held Keller fixed in this unnerving gaze.

"So" Jhoppa began softly "you're saying that you could make anything as a God could make it."

Keller's eyes widened. Some part of this mind realized this was not a question.

"Not me." Keller sputtered.

Jhoppa leaned closer and quickly pressed.

"Why not? You just said 'even if it took generations.' Why couldn't you, if you were the culmination of that learning?"

"I..." Keller couldn't decide what to do with his hands. He suddenly did not want to touch the scroll case. "But, I'm just..."

"Just?" Jhoppa snorted. "Just what? Mortal? What's the difference really?"

Keller shrank back a bit. He did not know what to make of Jhoppa's mood, which seemed no less jovial than usual yet threaded through with something frantic, seething.

Jhoppa seemed to notice his younger companion's fear and immediately sat back against his tree with a laugh and stoked the fire.

"Something to think about." he winked and said no more.

Keller did think about it. One week later on the trail, he finally answered Johppa's question.

"Mortal's die."

Jhoppa turned in his saddle to watch Keller catch him up.

"Exactly." Jhoppa jabbed the air.

Keller marveled that he needed no explanation whatever to pick up the conversation right where they'd left it a week before.

"I don't understand. Isn't that obvious?"

"Then why didn't you come up with it sooner?" Jhoppa snickered.

"I did. I just kept thinking because I thought you wanted a better answer."

"What's better than such succinct truth? Very powerful, remember that." he winked and continued. "But I do want a better answer.

"Mortal's die. God's don't. So how does that make one able to do things the other can't?"

Keller frowned.

"You mean why does that make gods able to do what mortals can't?"

Jhoppa shrugged.

"And the other way round, but that's really a different conversation altogether. Yes, let's go with the first thought." And he swept a hand before him as though expecting an answer right then.

"Well," Keller leaned forward over his saddle. "Gods live longer, I guess."

Jhoppa rolled his eyes.

"You're guessing such an obvious fact? I think you can safely assume that seventy or so years is coming a lot sooner than never. So gods live longer. So what?"

Keller huffed.

"So what? Isn't that enough?"

Jhoppa turned mockingly empty doe eyes on Keller.

"I'm just a poor, simple vagabond, my dear boy. You'll have to explain it to me in slow, easy words."

Keller snorted.

Jhoppa simply blinked blankly at him but could not hide the twinkle in his eye. He was still waiting for an answer.

Keller made no attempt to hide his exasperation.

"They have more...time...to do whatever it is gods do." Jhoppa egged him on infuriatingly. Keller played with his horse's mane.

"They...learn?" he glanced at his companion out of the corners of his eyes.

Jhoppa touched his own chest delicately.

"You're asking me?" No longer feigning ignorance, his eyes were filled with mischief.

"Fine. Alright." Keller pressed on. "If we're comparing the two - and I don't have any idea what gods do in their spare time..."

Jhoppa nearly unseated himself trying not to laugh. Keller had to ignore this to keep his thoughts from scattering. His voice grew stronger as he forged ahead.

"...so I can only use my own experience to compare."

Jhoppa's head snapped up and he pointed frantically from Keller to his nose and back with his mouth clenched tight as though denying himself speech. Keller frowned and continued.

"Then they have longer to learn, play, work," he was looking up and listing the things he thought of himself doing.

"Love," he trailed off suddenly and turned his face away.

They were both silent for a few moments.

"Do you think Gods love, Jhoppa?" Keller asked absently as his mind wandered back to Overlook and everyone he was close to there.

"Yes." Keller nearly missed Jhoppa's whispered answer.

Then after a few more heartbeats of silence, Jhoppa reached across and punched Keller in the arm to bring him back to the present.

"And all these things constitute..."

Keller looked confused.

"Experiences?" he shrugged.

Jhoppa touched his nose again but this time with a wink. Seeming satisfied, he sat back a bit in his saddle and relaxed.

"Have you ever noticed how some people can pack more into a few short years than others can in a whole lifetime?"

Keller considered this but, as he thought the question might be rhetorical, he was all too happy not to answer. The further they got down the trail without words the more relieved he became that he was right.

Destiny Calls and I let it go to voice mail
Blessed are these spikes beneath my feet
Springing into action, I fall nimbly on my face
This one's a bit too much but I'll revel in it anyway
Words escape me but then come flooding in too fast
I bet this is the last chance
And'll probly be my favorite too
Yeah, that's about right
I'll never see it through
But neither will you
So, let's see the truth of each other now
That's all we can do

The end:

Thanks for walking a while with me. May you find growth in adversity and love within and without. If you live in interesting times, may you share them with those you cherish and be seen for the glorious being that you are. You carry abundance. Act like it.

Please use the following pages to make your own wordy (or artsy) things about hope and grace. I would love to see them!

@this_is_essee
contact@this-is-essee.com
this-is-essee.com